RARE BIRD OF FASHION

ERIC BOMAN

RARE BIRD OF FASHION
The Irreverent Iris Apfel

with an introduction by Harold Koda
and an autobiographical text by Iris Apfel

WITH 169 ILLUSTRATIONS, 149 IN COLOUR

Thames & Hudson

Photographs pp. 11, 12, 13, 15, 16, 18, 25, 26–27, 28, 30, 31,
32–33, 34, 35, 36–37, 39 private collection of Carl and Iris Apfel;
p. 24 Edward Haleman. All other photography by Eric Boman.

The clothing featured in this book constitutes a private wardrobe
rather than a catalogued collection. The information in the plate descriptions
is therefore to the owner's best knowledge and dates given are approximate only.

First published in the United Kingdom in 2007
by Thames & Hudson Ltd, 181A High Holborn, London WC1V 7QX

Reprinted 2016

British Library Cataloguing-in-Publication Data
A catalogue record for this book is available from the British Library

ISBN 978-0-500-51344-6

Printed and bound in China by C&C Offset Printing Co. Ltd

To find out about all our publications, please visit **www.thamesandhudson.com**.
There you can subscribe to our e-newsletter, browse or download our current catalogue,
and buy any titles that are in print.

CONTENTS

Portrait of Iris Apfel in her absence

PREFACE

Nothing warms my heart like talent, and it has been the source of some of my life's most rewarding experiences. Seeing a picture, hearing a piece of music, entering a building or eating a plate of food have been among the many milestones — at times, even given me new direction. Ironically, this respect for talent also twisted my years as a fashion photographer somewhat out of shape, for I reveled more in an editor's knack for putting together the elements of an image than I worried about my own eventual imprint on the whole.

I knew nothing of Iris Barrel Apfel when I chanced upon an article in *The New York Times* about her much-discussed exhibition at The Costume Institute of New York's Metropolitan Museum of Art. Many great costume exhibitions have mixed scholarly insight with curatorial flair, but here was something else: the fact that the outfits were put together by their wearer added a realism that endowed them with a glowing gravitas, and the show as a whole with a rare emotional coherence. The rich opportunity for photography was an instant temptation, and, via Harold Koda, I contrived to meet Iris Apfel and present the idea for this book.

Luckily, Mrs. Apfel had a book on her wish-list — but the show was about to be packed up and shipped for storage at its next venue. Shortly after our first meeting (which could have been our hundredth), we embarked on the business of methodically and efficiently recreating the outfits for photography. The intensity of that process was spurred by our seeing eye to eye over every creative decision — as if we'd been on the road together for years.

Mrs. Apfel soon saw that a photograph is different from an exhibition or real life, and effortlessly made the adjustments. I was once again watching a great editor at work. By then, I had learned that this was indeed her *carrière manquée*.

A book of mannequins could have been dauntingly dry, and a voice was needed to breathe soul into the fiberglass dummies. Mrs. Apfel was full of stories that put everything we were playing with into perspective, and husband Carl had the snapshots to back them up. But stories told again and again become irrevocably shaped by their storyteller, and Mrs. Apfel likes hers just so. That's when she gently but firmly yanked away the legal pad on which I had scribbled some "key" questions for her. I never saw the pad again, but instead page after page in her florid hand, at tired times looking like early Twombly.

Sparked by one woman's ways of turning herself out, I've had the privilege of joining the Apfels on their colorful voyage through a lifetime of work and play. I hope that, even as the reader is looking at a dress on a dummy, this book will offer a whiff of sea air, the tinkle of an ice cube in a cocktail glass, the rhythm of a cha-cha, and the sound of laughter.

ERIC BOMAN

INTRODUCTION

When Oscar Wilde exhorted members of his public to "either be a work of art or wear a work of art," he was not considering those anomalous individuals who were, like himself, endowed with the confidence, imagination, and means to do both. He seems to propose that the donning of a couture masterpiece may be relied upon as a kind of default for those interested in an aestheticized allure. However, while a stylish distinction might be projected in the *mode à la mode*, it is most persuasively conveyed when fashion is individualized through clever interpretation — that is, when it is achieved through the suave coordination and novel juxtaposition of the various artful components of dress.

This book, in the spirit of Wilde's approach to personal style, and based on an exhibition of Iris Barrel Apfel's fashion collection that originated at The Costume Institute of the Metropolitan Museum of Art, not only presents works of intrinsic artistic merit but also a strategy of dressing that is in itself an artistic exercise. Amply sharing Mrs. Apfel's visual audacity and willingness to gild the lily is her collaborator Eric Boman. What collector and photographer also share is a visual sensitivity developed from an immersion in the history of the arts that prizes balance and conceptual clarity.

In the beginning, the exhibition was conceived as a rather modest representation of highlights of Mrs. Apfel's jewelry and fashion accessories. The addition of clothing was intended to provide a mere backdrop, but Mrs. Apfel's collection, which she refers to simply as her "closet," was so vast that the project quickly expanded to accommodate the full range of her holdings. In turn the emphasis shifted from the collection to the collector and her highly creative approach to dress. It was immediately clear that the styling of each ensemble should be given over to Mrs. Apfel herself. Who better to present this astonishingly eclectic assortment than the woman who had acquired it all, and wears it still with such panache?

For the past fifty years, Mrs. Apfel, as co-founder with her husband, Carl, of the textile house Old World Weavers, has had the opportunity to explore a wealth of souks, thrift shops, *marchés aux puces*, *maisons de couture*, and *petites mains* workshops. Given her determined preferences as well as the whimsy, fantasy, and exoticism that inform much of her sensibility, it is not surprising that distinct stylistic narratives emerge in her collection. Even seemingly mundane and everyday objects are transformed into artistic flourishes through the aesthetic complexity and self-assurance that define the Apfel style.

It has been observed that, like democracy itself, American style is a celebration of the individual, the independent, and even, on occasion, the eccentrically idiosyncratic. There is in the freewheeling American psyche an element of the adventurous that manifests itself in a disregard of conventional pieties, an impulse toward rule-breaking. Mrs. Apfel's casual pairing of a Stella Forest fur with an African wall hanging or a Bill Blass jacket with a Native

American dance skirt is characteristic of the slyly witty and irrepressible "anything goes" bravura of American style at its most imaginative.

Humor in dress is always a dangerously negotiated tightrope walk, but it is not surprising that the playful colors, buoyant shapes, and graphic patterning favored by Mrs. Apfel are so elegantly rendered since they reflect the technical finesse of James Galanos, Emanuel Ungaro, Ralph Rucci and Geoffrey Beene, among others. More unexpected is the virtuosity, unusual in a client or collector, that reveals itself when Mrs. Apfel jumbles and reassembles the carefully composed ensembles of her favorite couturiers.

Mrs. Apfel's combining of, say, a Lanvin haute couture "burnoose" with silver jewelry from the American Southwest is so estranged from authenticity that it exists as a poetic and gleeful evocation of an exotic other that is a completely imaginary construction. While much of the power of Orientalism in fashion resides in its ability to introduce erotic and fantastical narratives, this form of exoticism has also been characterized by anachronistic conflations and the introduction of Western elements to non-Western dress. But despite the submerged meanings and false readings inherent in such citation, there exists in its endorsement a proclamation of the value of indigenous dress over the inherently self-obsolescent cycle of Western fashion. It is in this way that Mrs. Apfel explores the seductive associations of regional dress and the vanishing beauty of its artisanal forms.

While she claims that during her workday she is likely to be found in her favorite fabric, denim, the reality is more complex. For, though Mrs. Apfel might combine sportswear elements into dressier ensembles, her favorite strategy for daywear is to take an outer coat by a tailoring master such as Gianfranco Ferré or Norman Norell and wear it alone as a dress.

Evening dresses are often characterized by sumptuous fabrics and exaggerated silhouettes. The pragmatics of daywear are set aside to maximize head-turning entrances and a visually arresting glamour. Eveningwear is a kind of masquerade in which one attempts to realize the fantasy of oneself. Mrs. Apfel's evening clothes, with their bold colors, emphatic shapes, and sensual materials, have a Fellini-esque theatricality. But it is in the fluttering surfaces of her favored feathered eveningwear that her status as *rara avis* is not only asserted but takes full flight.

Rara avis refers, of course, to the unusual distinction of Mrs. Apfel's personal style. Even in the flock of New York style setters, she stands apart as a rare bird. Mrs. Apfel, who has the gift of an "eye" that can ferret out treasures from a morass of flea-market junk and mark-down racks, is endowed with the yet rarer ability to collage objects of autonomously assertive beauty into compositions of a larger, unified whole. Her joy of the hunt has resulted in a collection of astonishing beauty, but it is in the incorporation of her treasures into her daily life that they take on a fuller conceptual richness.

HAROLD KODA
Curator of The Costume Institute,
Metropolitan Museum of Art, New York

A WORD, OR THREE OR FOUR

BY IRIS BARREL APFEL

The seeds of my so-called gift for wearing "everything and the kitchen sink" were unwittingly bestowed upon me at the very beginning — only in my case the kitchen sink was a laundry basket. I arrived on the planet before my crib was delivered. When the hospital called that late summer morning to announce that Mama would be coming home with bouncing baby Barrel some time that afternoon, what might elsewhere have caused household hysteria was handled with aplomb. Grandma marched to the utility room, grabbed the family laundry basket, and scoured and scrubbed it. She then hung it out on the washline to sun and dry. Just across the way, four-year-old Albie Kemp was looking out of his living-room window in amazement. What was Grandma doing? Why was the *basket* being hung out to dry? Albie's mother thought quickly and opined that the Barrels were expecting the stork to drop me off some time soon, and this was where I'd land. Albie, flushed with excitement at the prospect of being privy to so momentous a happening, promptly stood guard at the window. Nothing and no one could budge him — not breakfast, nor lunch, nor the promise of a new puppy dog. He was glued to his watch-post. That is, until 5.15, when his father arrived and pulled him away, kicking and screaming, to his dinner. A moment later I arrived. Albie missed it all and until he reached puberty never really forgave his father.

Early on, in an attempt to civilize me, I was given dancing lessons and elocution lessons and piano lessons and language lessons, and was even given deep religious training. It would have been far more productive for all concerned if the monies had gone directly to some great charitable cause, like a home for wayward girls in Uzbekistan or the famine in Armenia.

One day, when I was about eight years old, the doorbell rang and Lottie announced the arrival of my mother's most do-gooder friend, who had a passion for matchmaking — not lovers, but down-and-outers … with her friends' checkbooks. She had in tow a rather bedraggled but beautiful young man, who looked needy and seedy and sad. My heart went out to him immediately (Mother's purse took a little more time). He was a brilliant photographer, we were told, sent by divine intervention to record some of my early talents. That I couldn't carry a tune and danced like an elderly elephant never entered the equation. Mama eventually promised to transport me to the appointed studio the next afternoon.

The idea of being immortalized as a performing artist was really more than I could bear. I ran to consult with my Lottie, who was — I never mentioned — a *confidante extraordinaire*, housemaid and resident Father Diviner, who for almost ten years spent every waking moment in a vain attempt to convert my grandmother. That her artistic sensibilities played fifth fiddle to her cleaning skills didn't disturb me in the least.

The first item on the agenda was to find out which of the arts would give best expression to my "talents." After long discussion, we elected ballet as the most visually effective. I was swooning with joy and anticipation, until for the first time in my young life I encountered the eternal feminine panic: "I have nothing to wear." While our larder was overstuffed, our closets were bereft of tutus. Lottie had anticipated the problem and brought out "The Big Beautiful Book of Ballet Dancers," one of Mother's favorites. (Mother was a balletomane and began to drag me to high-powered performances at a very tender age.) We flipped the pages, and flipped again at the sight of Isadora Duncan in her diaphanous draperies. That was it! And it was a perfect choice, as Grandma had just bought a huge bolt of snow-white cheesecloth for some future cleaning job.

The next morning we fussed and cut and draped. At that point in my career, it has to be admitted, I was bumpy and lumpy in all the wrong places. I looked like a handful of clay that some amateur sculptor was about to fashion: he squeezed here, kneaded there, got bored, and went to lunch. I was hardly a figure of charm and nobody ever told me that diaphanous cheesecloth *n'existe pas*. I firmly believe to this day it was because of our disastrous line-for-line copy that I've never been able to cotton to Madame Grès. Undaunted, Lottie continued to style me. I was crowned with corkscrew curls and bottomed out with my black satin ballet slippers, which had long silk ribbons that crisscrossed what eventually became a pair of proper legs. Lottie looked at me and pronounced me Pavlova incarnate.

When Mama gazed upon the apparition that she had birthed, she almost dropped dead. "Oh my heavens," she wailed. "Cover your head." And she pushed me, police-style, into the waiting taxi. I couldn't fathom her chagrin as I thought I looked pretty swell. Eclectic, perhaps — but then *artistes* are allowed their eccentricities.

Me at three (or four or five) with my Uncle Harry

Once arrived at our destination, Mama realized the die was cast. Leaving her to trail me, I loped up two flights of rickety stairs and, appropriately, heard very sad music wafting out of the studio Victrola. It put me in the proper mood. I opened the door and with wild abandon flung myself against the dingy faded wall, assumed my "dying swan" position, and informed the bewildered creature behind the lens that I was indeed ready for my close-up.

I didn't realize it then, of course, but it was my very first flirtation with chic, with "avoir du chien" in the true, French sense — that is, daring, not caring what anyone would think, truly a persona of my own. I'd seen how, come hell or high water, one could bring forth a vision. That in this case it was an exercise in futility frankly mattered not at all. I thought it was all fabulous, and it was on that day, I now know, that I began my hopelessly lifelong love affair with style.

The family homestead was a large, many-level, red-brick house, undistinguished to behold, but for my grandparents it was the culmination of a dream. Grandpa had fled to America at the beginning of the new century when he received his conscription papers, leaving behind his dreaded Czar and his loving new wife who was not yet sixteen summers old. They had been married for less than a year, and she was already pregnant with my mother. Grandpa promised to work very hard and save his shekels and send her a ticket asap. Sure enough, when Mama was five months old, the anticipated ticket arrived and Grandma hurriedly left for Hamburg in the dead of night, having never been away from home before and speaking only Russian. It was all very "Fiddler on the Roof."

After a very lonely fortnight in Hamburg she and Mama were finally able to board the steamer. Two ghastly weeks later, having endured rough seas, inedible food and hideously cramped accommodation in steerage, they were reunited with Grandpa in New York City. Leaving the dock and the customs formalities, they boarded a broken-down horse cart and rode off into the sunset of their first lodgings, a tenement walk-up apartment on the umpteenth floor. Untutored and inexperienced as Grandpa was, he nonetheless possessed an innate flair and had put together his tiny love nest with "more dash than cash," as they say in the trade. Grandma was delighted and set about her endless cleaning, marketing and sewing almost immediately. I think she used up all the family's housewifely genes in one generation, as Mama and I received nary a one.

Grandpa was a master tailor — he made the most splendiferous buttonholes — and plied his trade morning, noon, and night in a valiant and successful effort to buy the tickets that would bring almost everyone who shared his blood to America. In the process he collapsed and was warned by the doctors that, if he fancied the idea of a ripe old age, he had to slow down, move away from the frenzy of tenement life, and seek seclusion in the fresh air of the countryside. On the double the entire family, now numbering four with Uncle Ben, boarded a little boat and set off for the pastoral shores of Queensboro. They landed in Long Island City and became early settlers of the area, living on a little farm with a nanny goat and part-ownership of a cow, and had to cross the river back and forth once a week to buy their provisions. Each forage was a full day's journey: the bridge to Manhattan wasn't opened until around 1910.

Mama, crisp and precise ...

By the time I came about, the family was happily settled in Astoria, the residential section of Long Island City, on the edge of the East River, gazing across at the bright lights of Manhattan. Astoria was a mostly blue-collar neighborhood. At some point during my growing up, my mother felt it would be better for my future status if I got out of the backwaters and was sent to a finer school, with more "elegant" surroundings and friends, and a greater chance of admission to an Ivy League college. My father would have none of it. He was adamant. He fussed and fumed and Mama soon realized she was dealing with a definite no-no. I was no better, he explained, than the Spanish baker's son or the immigrant Chinese restaurant owner's daughter or the African-American bricklayer's brother. America was full of all kinds of people who came in all kinds of colors and creeds, and if I really wanted to succeed in this world, I had better meet them all and understand what they were all about. It made good sense to me then and I shall never stop thanking him for that sound and sensible lesson. One up for Daddy-O.

… and Daddy-O, throwaway chic.

Dad was a man who knew everything about some things and something about everything. Totally unconventional, he was a mass of contradictions. He constantly read Shakespeare and the philosophers, but he dearly loved a good crapshoot as well. He had the courage of his convictions and cared not a fig for outside approval. He taught me to spot a phony at ten paces and saw to it that I learned to read the right-hand side of a menu. He was also a senior-grade market freak and ardent traveler, who knew the price of cheese in every European capital city. He paid no attention to what he wore, but he had a natural sense of style and always looked marvelous in clothes. Though he had to be lassooed into dressing up, when he did all the ladies found him stunning. But he had eyes only for Mother, and he adored her until the day he died.

Mama was in many ways quite his opposite: conventional and concerned about what people would think. Ahead of her time, she graduated from college and went to law school. Brilliant in business, she refused the use of a calculator lest it "dim her wits," and talked to her stockbrokers every single day until she died three weeks after her hundredth birthday. She was always groomed and coiffed, band-box perfect, even early in the morning. That drove this messy teenager quite mad. Mama had a great reputation as a fashion plate and worshiped at the Altar of the Accessory. She taught me how one could transform a bargain-basement little nothing of a dress and transport it to fashion heaven. Never was there anyone who could do such wonders with a scarf. My style turned out to be quite different from hers but it was she who laid my groundwork and she eventually became my closest and dearest friend (she had a staggering sense of humor and told the best off-color jokes). Mama never kept house, as we lived in a kind of family compound where Grandma ruled the roost. Whenever I'd visit my stay-at-home aunties, who could cook and bake and sew beautiful dresses, I'd invariably say, "Oh Auntie, you're so special, you can do all of these wonderful things; all my mother knows how to do is make money!"

I must have been twelve or thirteen when Mama opened her first boutique. These were still Depression years and doing business was tough. Mama worked long hard hours, which left little time for me. Although I confess I resented it at first, I know now it made me into the self-reliant world-class shopper I am. Being a pragmatist even then, I understood that if I wanted clothes I'd have to ferret them out on my own.

My first solo shopping spree was a bit scary. Easter was a-coming and Mama thought I should have a new outfit that was parade-worthy. We discussed strategy and the bottom line, and I ended up with $25 in my hot little hand. I set out for Manhattan and the famous discount store S. Klein on Union Square. Once there I fell madly in love with a silk tie-print shirtmaker dress: big poet sleeves, glorious buttons, trapunto-like collar and cuffs. I was smitten but resisted, recalling Mama's admonition: "Never buy the first thing you see. Always comparison shop." So off I went uptown to the bustling 34th Street area and, with insane zeal, scoured all the leading department stores. I found nothing I liked as well and panicked. What if someone else fancied "my" dress and made off with it? I hurried back downtown but couldn't locate my prey. After twenty minutes of agony I found it on another rack. I gave thanks to God Almighty and $12.95 to the cashier. I was delirious. Down the street I bought beautiful shoes at A. S. Beck for $3.95 and picked up a smashing straw hat. I was well under budget. Mama praised my good taste, Daddy my sense of value; the only dissent came from Grandpa's view of the buttonholes....

Emboldened by my recent success I began to forage seriously all around Manhattan. I was especially enchanted with Greenwich Village, then still bohemian, artsy, and romantic. My favorite spot belonged to a certain Mr. D'Aras, an elderly courtly gentleman who always wore a pince-nez and spats, and always treated me like a mini duchess. He encouraged my poking about and I think that my youthful interest in his faux treasures amused him no end. He was very kind and sold me my very first accessory — a brooch with a high gilt crown, lacy and cage-like, embedded with rhinestones. Cartier couldn't have pleased me more. Mr. D'Aras sold it to me for 65 cents.

Papa, at this point in my teens, had gone back into his family business of glass and mirror. He was quite expert in all manner of unusual and difficult installation and was much in demand by the top-drawer designers and architects of the day. The great, and maybe the first, interior decorator Elsie de Wolfe, or Lady Mendl as she liked to be known, was commissioned by Conrad Hilton to do an entire floor of what were to become elegant, expensive suites at the

Plaza Hotel in New York City. She took one for her own use and engaged Daddy-O to do all of the mirrorwork, on the condition that every Sunday he would personally instal the tricky stuff. She had enormous style and was surrounded by beautifully designed objects. As a bonus she had an adorable poodle called Blu Blu (I've always thought she must have dipped him into some solution of indigo). Anyhow one day Dad asked if he could bring me to view all this splendor. The following Sunday I entered a new and enchanted world. I was ushered into her fabulous *chambre à coucher*, where she graciously received from her bed, Blu Blu at her side. He jumped down to welcome me, took a sniff, and gave me a big kiss. I was in. We had a wonderful time and I received a permanent invitation to visit for the duration of the job. It was winter and she always wore a bedjacket; a different one on each visit. Always the same style but always made of different fur: chinchilla, mink, broadtail, sable. She had given Maximilian, the great furrier, a simple flannel number off the peg from Sears Roebuck and he copied it line for line. She taught me many things and spoke of her life and her business. I'll never forget a large bowl of the reddest, fattest apples that sat at the end of her bed, or the eighteenth-century make-up table filled with little pots of wax-like colored make-up. Much of what I absorbed on these visits lay fallow for years. It wasn't till later that I realized just how much I had learned from her about real-life style and how closely related fashion and interior design are.

On the beach, with a killer accessory

As an Art History major at New York University I quite naturally entered the art school of the University of Wisconsin when I transferred there, unaware that it was the most provincial department on campus. Mr. Varnum, ex-tombstone engraver, was the head honcho. He decided that, as it was the "machine age," it made sense for all his students to learn to draw with instruments, and he herded us off to the engineering school. I would not have recognized a piston if I fell on one, let alone a cross-section thereof. Without the "unauthorized" help and drawings of two darling fledgling male engineers, I'd still be sitting it out in Madison on the shores of Lake Mendota.

I took to perusing the Course Catalog to come up with something offbeat where I could earn some substitute credits. "Museum Administration 1" sounded appealing. I set off to meet with the instructor. I hadn't a clue as to the nature of the studies, and the dear little man giving the class didn't have one either. He almost collapsed when I appeared and declared me the first candidate in six years to apply. We discussed the situation and saw the solution. It was his dream, he said, one day before he left this vale, to create a small museum dedicated to indigenous American culture. "How about jazz?" I asked, as I was already several years into that scene. I'd always felt that jazz was design improvisation and worked on the same principles as interior decor and fashion construction: rhythm, mixing the high and the low, combining ethnic with classical elements. He loved the idea and said to go to work on a paper. I left his office on cloud nine and floated to the library, but it was 1940 and there was not *one* book on the subject. How I agonized.

The fates provided, however, and several days later I read in the local press that the great Duke Ellington was coming to town. "I have nothing to lose," I thought. "Let me go and see if I can get an audience with him." I remember to this day what I was wearing: gray flannel trousers with a matching cashmere sweater, goodlooking loafers, and a Cornell University blazer a beau had given me (white flannel piped with wine red, beautiful buttons, and the Cornell seal on the pocket). When I got backstage at the theatre, I knocked. The musician Ray Nance opened the door … and his eyes popped. "Lordy, lordy, who's your tailor?" he cried. "Come on in."

Ray introduced me to all the guys in the band and to the Duke himself, the most elegant man alive. We talked and talked and talked. The band was leaving on the milk train the next night for another gig on the South Side of Chicago and suggested I meet them there, as dozens of the now-legendary jazz greats would be in town and available for me to interview. It was an opportunity I couldn't miss, and I garnered enough original information to do an A-plus paper and to forge a future friendship with the Duke.

A night on the town in 1943: a beau, moi, the Duke and Billie Holiday

After all that jazz I was due to go back to Wisconsin but decided that, while I was in Chicago, I'd do some shopping. Mama, occupied with other matters, was often in arrears with my allowance. Now fortunately I was in possession of four weeks' worth. Flush, I decided to go uptown to Marshall Field's and buy myself a turban and a pair of large hoop earrings. I thought they would whoop up the blue denim jeans I'd taken to wearing. Those jeans were the most difficult article of clothing I'd ever lusted after. Unless you were a lumberjack or a field hand, or Paul Bunyan himself, nobody in Wisconsin wore them. But when I'm really after something I'm like a dog with a bone. I drove the male staff at the local Army & Navy store bananas — "Don't you know, Miss, ladies don't wear jeans? No, we don't have small sizes. No, we can't cut a large pair down," etc., etc. But I prevailed. After several weeks the proprietor, desperate to get me out of his hair, mail-ordered me a pair of boy-size denims. It was wonderful. At any rate, on my way to the millinery department in Marshall Field's I got waylaid at the book shop, where there were two huge tables laden with volumes of English and American poetry. I knew nothing about either. Thanks to my incurable curiosity, two hours later I was twelve books richer and all the loot was gone. "Better to put something *in* my head than *on* my head," I reasoned. It was another great lesson, which I urge every *jeune fille* to heed.

As a starry-eyed *Vogue* aficionado, I spent my senior year at university determinedly fantasizing over the prospect of winning the prestigious *Vogue Prix de Paris*, whose first prize was a year-long job in the Paris office. I gathered I was being seriously considered when they sent me a ticket to come from Madison to New York for a final interview, but something went wrong and that came to an end. I wasn't too perturbed as the office closed anyhow due to the war.

At the time I believed that fashion was my real passion, and I craved to play a part on its editorial side. I took a job at *Women's Wear Daily*, in those days strictly a trade publication, its offices located in a creepy old building on West 12th Street. Given the exalted position of "copy girl," I kept telling myself it was a noble thing to start at the bottom — and, baby, you couldn't get any lower. At least I had the chance to work my way up. As super-technology hadn't yet reared its ugly head, and there were only a couple of pneumatic tubes in the joint, it was my duty to run back and forth from desk to desk, up and down the stairs from department to department, delivering hot news and hot copy from editor to editor. My paycheck was pitiful, the ambience was frenzied, and I learned almost nothing of the business, but it kept me in great shape! After several months I realized my magazine editor's skills would never take root here, as a job vacancy was not likely to come up: the female editors were all a little too mature for maternity leave, yet not quite ripe enough for retirement.

Moving on, I had a fast rise to the very top, literally: I found myself in a stunning penthouse office, directly across the street from Saks Fifth Avenue. I had landed a glamour job as Girl Friday to Robert Goodman, who at that time was the leading men's fashion illustrator, doing major pages in *Esquire* and almost every top-drawer account he could handle. My duties were delicious and different every day, which suited me fine. My boss was a yum-yum who often would send me tootin' around town, scouting locations for his pictures. R.G. loved the high life, so I was able to get to spots otherwise off-limits to the likes of *moi*. Though he was very happily married, he loved women — especially interesting and/or beautiful ones. In those days in New York City they were plentiful and the studio was always full up.

It was there that I met Elinor Johnson, a beauteous, brainy babe, who was "slightly" engaged at that time to Jack Heinz and his 57 varieties. She had the brilliant idea of buying co-ops or taking long-term leases at the Marguery and the Louis Sherry, two tony buildings on Park Avenue, and furnishing them to the nines. Each was designed for a particular personality and a special lifestyle, like "kept woman," "visiting Hollywood producer," "playboy," etc. Through Jack's connections, she sold them all quite easily. The problem was decorating them in great style, what with the war raging, and furniture and fabrics difficult to obtain. We cruised junk yards and flea markets and remnant shops, and went crazy with mirror and chintz and daring paint colors. Elinor's big idea was to film what we were doing and how we did it, as it was a total improvisation. I was hired to write the script. The film was then to be sold and shown to women's groups, home economy classes and design schools, demonstrating how, using courage and imagination, you could put a smashing interior together with the limited materials at hand. When the film was finished, the guys on the decorating job begged Elinor to keep me on and she happily agreed. Spending at least twelve hours a day amidst the posh of Park Avenue in the '40s was very much to my taste and my friends all wondered how I would survive coming back to blue-collar Astoria for the remaining twelve. Thank heaven, I've always been very adaptable. I remained with Elinor through several apartments, and realized I had found my calling. Interior design was truly for me. It was bye-bye to fashion.

I realized that, while I was able to express myself in fantasy, Hollywood producers and kept women were hardly a part of my world, and I had better learn to be more practical. I therefore took a job with a small but highly regarded firm that specialized in offices and other types of commercial space, as well as very contemporary residential interiors. It was never my aesthetic but I bravely muddled away.

Mixing hot colors in an attempt to raise the temperature on an unheated site

My early, and enduring, design sensibilities: Venice and the Settecento, painted furniture, and fabulous fabrics

As World War II continued to rage, there was one place that became an absolute Mecca: Grossinger's, queen of all the resorts in the Catskill Mountains' fabled Borscht Belt. Though it's now a decrepit legend, I can attest to its glory days. Artists and writers, playboys and politicos, everybody who was anybody in the arts, media, fashion and entertainment (as well as many who lived in the Real World) came by to roost.

Into this manmade La La Land I tumbled via a job as editor/writer of Grossinger's daily newspaper. It started out as a two-week replacement gig but I made the grade and they invited me to remain at the inkpot. The best part for me was interviewing and commenting upon the hordes of celebrities who came and went. Every weekend the comedian Milton Berle would visit his mother, the original showbusiness mom. Sammy Davis, Jr. was there. Even Jerry Lewis....

The staff was expected to look as attractive as possible at all times but to make a special effort every evening. Playing dress-up was great fun for me and I began to experiment — to mix and match, to wear something I'd worn one day in another way the next. In order to expand my wardrobe I had to be inventive on a daily basis.

Every top-drawer designer in the Big Apple came to the Big G. I began to get noticed. One by one they would approve of my get-ups. We'd chat briefly and they'd say how delighted they would be to see me in their designs. I'd demur and say nothing could please me more, but that I was just a poor working girl. The reaction was always the same: "Don't worry. When you're back in the city, come up and we'll get it for you wholesale." As my appetite for couture grew way ahead of my paltry paycheck, it was an offer I couldn't refuse.

Monday was "Relax in Slacks" night but, for the other six, dress-up was de rigueur. It was an "if you got it, flaunt it baby" mentality. The best-dressed women were the trophy wives of two of the Kings of Seventh Avenue. One was a baby-doll, the other a slinky siren. They mainly wore Norman Norell and looked marvelous. I'd ogle them from afar but I couldn't learn anything, as I wasn't either of these types. (By the by, when I became an interior designer I did homes for both of them.) I'd never seen so much *luxe* in one place at one time. One of our long-term lady guests had a fetish for wristwatches and every night seemed to relish showing off a new one. I once asked her to tell me the time. She looked down at her stone-studded timepiece and answered, "It's five diamonds past eight rubies!" Her buxom lady friend was equally emblazoned. When I admired the dazzling display of jewelry on her overstuffed person, she confided modestly that these were only her Tuesday diamonds.... I soon realized that money alone could not buy good taste and that what you spent did not necessarily determine the success of an outfit. If you knew what to do, however, having *beaucoup* bucks couldn't hurt. As I had no Sugar Daddy waiting in the wings, I redoubled my efforts to look and experiment.

Life went along at a la-de-da pace. I worked hard and met wonderful, interesting people and learned in a relatively short time valuable lessons it would have taken me many years to accumulate anywhere else. But I was beginning to feel as though I had sat too long on the periphery of a big mad party. The war was finally over, thank God. VJ Day had come and gone, and it was now time to go home to Reality … and a shot at interior design.

I don't collect clothes, I buy them to wear. I do, however, collect many things, like the Native Americana here, Qing Dynasty costumes, Neapolitan pastori,
dog portraits, opaline glass, antique textiles, vintage handbags, shoe heels, strange chairs, etc., etc. – some the subjects of major museum exhibitions

This decision took more nerve than brain, as I had not the vaguest idea of running a business. But everything I ever do that's important is done via the gut: going into business, getting married, starting Old World Weavers, putting on exhibitions, writing this text, embellishing myself every day.

Over the course of time I had vaguely mentioned to a few interested guests that I yearned to practice decorating on my own. They all seemed to listen intently (there wasn't anything else to do at that moment) but I never thought that they paid serious attention. Fortunately, I was mistaken. A month or so after I set up shop, the phone began to ring.

I couldn't believe it then and I find it equally difficult to believe now that these kind, generous, otherwise mentally sound folk would chance working on something as important as a home with a twenty-something newcomer bereft of tangible credentials. Somehow they believed in me, and chose me, they said, because they liked the way I threw myself together. "The aesthetic was on target." They reasoned that if I could manage to make *moi* attractive, I should be able to do the same for a room. Such a leap of faith from them deserved a home-run hit from me.

The first of my new clients was … a Hollywood producer (of the "Hop-Along Cassidy" films), who had traded the high life of cigars and aspirins for full-blown vegetarianism and a house on Long Island. I did a complete job and it was so successful his wife immediately went into the interior decorating business. I was quite flattered.

Camping it up on an over-the-top display at a trade fair in Brussels

Darling ditzy Mrs D. was my very favorite. A fashion victim from her bleached blond beehive to her ankle-strapped platforms, this helpful dip had a big heart, a big following, and a much bigger mouth. Happily for me her friends had big ears and they all listened attentively to their leader.

The newly minted designer in a pensive moment

It started out as an unimportant commission — a one-bedroom, budget apartment in Brooklyn — but it was soon to rocket me smack into the middle of the postwar building boom that was suburbia. We mixed color with love and wit in that small apartment and the resulting ambience was striking and as much fun as Mrs. D. herself. She was delirious with the result and dragged each and every gal pal to gaze upon my creation. They agreed with their boss that it was "masterful" and promised — on pain of banishment — to recommend me highly to anyone they knew in need of my brand of social service.

The day soon came when Mrs. D. and her husband decided to join the exodus out of Brooklyn and follow the pack to the Promised Land, Long Island. I was summoned to behold a really lovely, sprawling, three-bedroom ranch house in a very upscale gated community. "Do you like it?" said she. "I love it," said I. "Then it's yours to do and I'll give you carte blanche … well, almost."

When I'd finished the job, I spent the day icing champagne and setting out *hors d'œuvres*, arranging flowers and lighting candles. When I saw the limo pull up, I stepped out the back door. An hour later I arrived home, happy but wiped out. The phone was ringing off the proverbial hook. "I love it, I love it!" Madame shrieked. "It's perfection. All is wonderful … but," she wailed, "you made one major mistake." Oh God, what could I possibly have overlooked? "Well," said she, "You know those gorgeous bookshelves in my gorgeous green liberry [sic]? You didn't even buy me one book! What will I put on the shelves? Fill 'em up, fill 'em up. I want 'em full." How stupid of me not to realize she didn't own a single book. I composed myself. "I didn't know what *kind* of books you might want." "Green ones, of course," she said. "All green." I was humbled. "Well, how many do you want?" "Just a minute, I'll measure." She came back, counting. "At least 90 running feet of them." For the next two weeks I camped out at Barnes & Noble.

I first went to Europe in 1952 or '53 with my parents, and after that with Carl, whom I'd married in '48. We always went by sea, until the liners stopped sailing. We weren't ever keen on flying, but then it's a long and tiring swim. I soon realized that if you went on the American ships, you were at home until you stepped off the boat at your destination. When you sailed the Italian Line, on the other hand, you were in Italy the minute you crossed the gangplank. And how happy that made me feel! If only I could speak the language … at least a word, or three or four. I determined to learn. Lacking time for proper study, I bought every Italian children's book I could find and soon became very proficient in "Pinocchio." From the advertising pages in the fabric magazines I learned Textilese. I then progressed to menus, most important of all. If you don't eat you can't work, *vero?* I never learned to conjugate and lost all my tenses. But then humor goes a long way with the Italians, so I felt free to speak. I did it my way … with courage and no verbs.

"FRANCE"

Captain Camille MAHÉ
and
Chief Purser Paul ERMEL
request the honour of
Mr. & Mrs Carl APFEL 's company
for cocktails, on Saturday, June 20th 1970
at 7.45 p.m.
in the Monaco Lounge - Verandah Deck

R.M.S. MAURETANIA. West Indies Cruise. 1959

FRENCH LINE

*"Getting there
was half the fun."*

T/n MICHELANGELO

UNITED STATES LIN.

COCKTAILS

		Per glass $
AMERICANO		.65
BACARDI		.70
BLOODY MARY		.75
CHAMPAGNE		.65
CUBA LIBRE		.80
DAIQUIRI		.70
DRY MARTINI		.75
LIQUEURS		.80
MANHATTAN		.65
NEGRONI		.50
ROB ROY		.75
ROSE		.65
RUSTY NAIL		.90

Cocktails made with Bourbon Whisky
Extra charge $ .20

VARIOUS DRINKS

		Per glass $
EGG NOGG BRANDY		.80
EGG NOGG RUM		.75
GIN FIZZ		.60
MILK PUNCH		.65
OLD FASHIONED		.70
PIMM'S N° 1 CUP		.65
PLANTERS PUNCH		.75
PUNCH CREOLE		.65
TOM COLLINS		.65
WHISKY SOUR		.70
CITRONNADE		.15
ORANGEADE		.15
SIROPS NIGERIA		.15

My transatlantic traveling companion, Carl, is my favorite fella; my darling, my balance, my Rock. Our courtship was a whirlwind of holidays. First date Columbus Day, proposal Thanksgiving, ringed and blinged Christmas Eve, wed on Washington's birthday, and our glorious glamorous honeymoon on Palm Beach was over on St. Patrick's Day. How green were we!

Our values, our politics, and our tastes almost always jive. He can do so many things I can't do that he makes me feel complete. He's charming and caring and cuddly and cute, and he can even cook Chinese. What more could a girl want? But best of all he makes me laugh. Really laugh a lot. For an antique I'm considered to be fairly hip but I admit to being, when it comes to marriage, an old-fashioned square. After all it's been more than half a century and I still have the same old husband and, by the by, the same old face!

Old Twinkle Toes and me, kicking up our heels at my former stomping-ground, good old Grossinger's

In the early '50s Carl and I began our business, Old World Weavers. We specialized in weaving exact reproductions of antique period fabric. Our clients were the rich and famous, and we did tons of historic restoration projects, like major work in the White House during the combined reigns of nine presidents. Because of business we spent almost three months of every year traveling the world to find offbeat classic period textile designs and to locate specific mills with specialized techniques to replicate them properly. They were exciting and challenging years.

I've always been extremely grateful to have traveled during that period and to have experienced the last of the "Old World." One was still able to find highly skilled artisans to carry out any wild idea that dropped into one's head – and surely they did, and often. I guess I've been a closet designer who could never sew or cut, but I had some ideas and I could sketch. God knows I had all the fabric and the trimmings. It isn't easy to design an outfit and trying my hand at it gave me an everlasting respect for the artistry and craftsmanship of the true couturier. Nevertheless I had my fling with dressmakers, bagmakers and shoemakers. Whenever someone would admire the fabric on a finished piece and ask where it came from, my husband would say, "Thank you! I just shot my couch."

At the beginning, the Old World Weavers' showroom was a suitcase, which Carl lugged around during his lunch hour to test the market. As I kept designing, the bag kept expanding. Finally, in an effort to condense, I got rid of many gorgeous heavy silk dupioni taffeta samples because they weighed a ton, and replaced them with one very long blanket – 14 inches of graded colors. Most attractive. By then Carl had secured an appointment with the iconic decorator Dorothy Draper. She was a rather large woman, who received him from behind a rather large trestle table. In a dramatic gesture Carl threw the new blanket in front of her and she gasped. "This is what I've looked for all my life, young man. This is the first intelligently scaled stripe I've ever seen. I'm doing a job for a colonel who has this marvelous house in the Bahamas with enormously high windows and I need horizontal stripes which I have not been able to find. Can you make me 300 yards?" The following day we had a visit from retailing legend Sarah Fredericks, who placed an order for another 250. With these two great tastemakers in our corner, we took it as a go-ahead.

Our first real showroom was in New York City on East 57th Street, in the middle of all the best antique dealers, but you had to walk up three double flights of stairs. It was "starting at the top" all right – not the greatest thing when there's no elevator. Nevertheless it didn't seem to matter to the "ladies who lunch," Mrs. Marjorie Merriweather Post among them. She had the smarts to wear sneakers for the climb and eventually became a very good client.

Early one morning the telephone rang. "This is Mrs. Post and I must speak with Mr. Apfel immediately." "Oh my God," I cried. "What happened?" Carl took the phone and Mrs. Post said, "Mr. Apfel, last night my draperies were delivered. They are absolutely stunning. They're hanging in my sitting room and I'm on top of an 18-foot ladder examining them. You have also made me exquisite silk fringe but I *must* know, how many little balls are there supposed to be in a running yard?" My husband thought for a minute and he said, "Mrs. Post, every day I eat your raisin bran. Can you tell me please how many raisins I'm supposed to find in a tablespoon?" "Touché, Mr. Apfel," she replied. "My God, I'm a foolish woman and I'd better get down from this ladder before I break my neck. I love the stuff and that's all that matters!"

A costly coat for Carl

Talking of loving "stuff," my very first fashion-house visit was a birthday gift from Sydney Gittler, resident fashion genius at Ohrbach's (he pioneered line-for-line copies of great European couture originals). It was a Balenciaga "opening." We were in the front row, with all the attendant fuss. I felt like I'd died and gone to heaven.

My personal shopping, however, had nothing to do with the shows. I went to the end-of-season sales and, later, as I became a "steady," I got into the *cabines.* My first purchase was the orangey-red Lanvin coat with the big cockade [see p. 143, left], at so puny a price that I blush to recount it. Anyway, I chose it, along with a magnificent, heavy, black satin cape. When they asked where to send them, I hesitated because we were shortly leaving Paris, and was flabbergasted when they suggested they deliver them to the ship. That year we were boarding in Naples, but the charming *vendeuse* said, "*Aucun problème*, Madame. They will be in your state room when you arrive at Cannes." Unbelievably, there they were, trussed up in a gorgeous labeled box, tied with silk ribbons. What a thrill! And, best of all, no delivery charges. Those were the days....

Chez Estée Lauder, client and friend

Early on I was very taken with the style of Pauline de Rothschild, both for her person and her environments. She was bold and gutsy and chic, chic, chic!

But I admired Millicent Rogers much more because her taste went all over the map: Balenciaga to Navajo skirts back to Salzburg and Austrian peasants. She had a wardrobe I lusted after. There

Mother ready for a high-seas gala

is in Taos, New Mexico, a wonderful small museum named for her, and it features, among many other things, her collection of Native American jewelry. She had the loot and the wit to get all the great stuff from the chiefs themselves. There is one necklace in the collection that knocks my socks off. It's heavy and huge — chunks of irregular pieces of turquoise, seemingly strung in a haphazard fashion, but believe me: pure dynamite! Whenever I'm anywhere in the state of New Mexico, I make a pilgrimage to coo over this great hunk of stuff.

I blush to admit that I was at one point very much taken with Rosalind Russell and her career woman get-ups, long before the movie versions of *Gypsy* and *Auntie Mame*. I don't remember if she did the original show on Broadway, but I do remember turning black and blue from all the poking at me during the performance. I sat between Carl and a good gentleman friend, and every time Mamie re-appeared in another dazzling get-up, they would prod me and yell, "That's perfect for you. Get one like it!"

On the other hand, most of the women on the Best Dressed List made me yawn....

There was, however, an important influence that came from a peculiar place. One rainy morning while lost on the streets of Brooklyn I unexpectedly turned a corner, which literally and figuratively led to a new chapter in my history.

With my Tunisian hostess, Fawzia Gherab

I found myself at a strange-looking emporium, where a scene of unimaginable chaos greeted me. It could have been a Syrian souk. On the selling floor there were skillions of plain pipe racks overburdened with garments; no dressing rooms; women of all shapes and sizes in varying shades of undress, pulling and grabbing the garments in an effort to try them on in plain view. It was in this bedlam that I found and bought my first affordable American couture. Upstairs, the Back Room was, for me, an Aladdin's cave. Never before could I have dreamed of owning a Norman Norell, a Trigère or a Ben Zuckerman.

The establishment was the brainchild of Mrs. Loehman, Saint of Seventh Avenue, whose shrewd snapping-up of samples, rejects and overstock garments during the Depression saved many a brilliant designer from financial collapse. She paid ready cash, which she carried in a long black miser's purse beneath her long black skirt. She resold her treasures at rock-bottom prices in her zany zoo of a shop. It was very out of the way for me but I made it a habit to visit on occasion. Often I had no time for trying on the clothes but with those ridiculous prices and sensational couture fabrics I'd think, "What the hell. If they don't fit, I'll make pillows."

Mrs. Loehman was sometimes in residence, looking like something out of Toulouse-Lautrec, with her gray topknotted hair, round rouge spots and high-buttoned shoes. She would sit on a tall stool, as though umpiring a tennis match, and look out on the floor, surveying her acolytes. One day she called me over. "I've been watching you," said she. "You're certainly no beauty but you have something much much better. You have style." Though I was flattered by her attention I didn't know quite what she meant, and truthfully until I began to scribble this text I never actually took the time to analyze it.

In the souk: just as much fun as shopping at Loehman's

Style is quite impossible to define, but I'll give it a go. Like charisma, you know it when you see it. Not too many possess it: unlike fashion, it cannot be bought. Imaginative, one of a kind, it differs from individual to individual. It's an offshoot of personality, not a cover-all, and it's concerned with real life, not just high fashion. Sometimes it seems to belong more to street people than to the *haut monde*, as it often grows out of a lack of material things. Most importantly, it must be real — yours — not a slavish copy of someone else's. Studying yourself to learn who you really are can be painful but it's crucial to be curious, as style can become a creative solution for personal shortcomings. It's wonderful to do your own thing — that is, *if* you have a thing to do. If you don't, take the sage advice of Harold Koda, who cautions, "Don't try this at home." It's always best to be yourself. For me it's a tough balancing act. You have to care deeply and at the same time not give a damn. True style implies attitude, attitude, attitude. It's elusive, exclusive, ephemeral: therein lies its magic.

ENDÔME PARIS

MARRAKECH · OUARZAZATE · TI...URT SKOURA

*"To market, to market
to buy a fat pig.
Home again, home again,
dancing a jig."*

A Bulògna à s pò magnar
própri in mod particular
del lasagn a la bulgnêisa
i filet a l'ulandêisa
e i turtlein bein pein e zâl
sôul da Zurla al "Papagal"

ristorante
"al pappagallo,,
bologna - piazza mercanzia, 3 - tel. 232-807
proprietari fratelli zurla

I've been accused of liberating and inspiring hordes of women of every age to have more courage in dressing and not to be afraid of experimentation. If it works for you, I'm delighted: I shall have done something for the common good. But if it's a chore or no fun, forget it. I'd hate to give rise to a new generation of fashionistas looking like plastic mannequins or Yetta Samovar.

Mirror, mirror, on the wall … @*&%!

Wit and humor are key components to my philosophy of dressing. Never take yourself or an outfit too seriously. "Outside of the box" has always been "inside my bag," and it's taken me to some very strange places. For instance, I'm big on the animal kingdom. I have a multi-tiered silver necklace which belonged to a little white horse and was worn at a wedding ceremony in the south of India [see p. 149]. "If it's good enough for the horse," I thought, "it's good enough for me." And once at a Parisian flea market I came upon some very large and extraordinary-looking silver pieces. In my fractured French, I asked, "What's that?" "Jewelry for an elephant," came the reply. "I'll have it," said I. "Madame has an elephant?" "Of course!" I cried. "Everyone in New York has an elephant!" I then fell in love at a Florida fair with a small metal purse in the shape of a dog [see p. 74]. Upon closer inspection I discovered one of his male components was missing, which enabled me to secure a far better price (sex rearing its lovely head).

In the early '50s, when a flea market was really a flea market, I rummaged about a lot. Sometimes textile dealers had huge stocks that interested me, sometimes just the sleeve of a dress. One day at the *marché aux puces* I found a priest's tunic. It was ruby silk velvet, and down the front was a large inset of a beautiful silk broché with marvelous braiding. Carl took a fit. "You don't need any old clothes!" he fumed. I had to have it. There was a scene. Thankfully heaven provided. The fashion guru Eugenia Sheppard of the *Herald Tribune* happened to waddle past and say, "How gorgeous, how glorious." I said, "Please go and tell my husband who you are and how stunning this is." She did and I got it. I made some matching trousers and slippers, too. (The outfit came in very handy when attending various black-tie dos at the White House. During the oil shortage under the Nixon administration one always froze to death.)

A decade later, I was stuck in traffic in a taxi with Carl, going down the rue du Faubourg Saint-Honoré in Paris. Out of the window I spied a photographer carrying equipment in one hand, and an incredible hat and coat in the other. It was the first time I'd ever seen Tibetan lamb.

On a hair high

In my Norell Smoking with a fat Fu dog as minaudière

I was intrigued. "Stop the car!" I jumped out and pursued the poor guy. He went to Lanvin. I followed him into the elevator. It turned out he had borrowed the outfit for a shoot. "I must have that coat," I drooled to the *vendeuse*. She apologized profusely, saying it was for a show, but that they could order me one if I liked. "I'm leaving tonight and I must have it." I carried on so, they gave it to me. Wearing that coat, with its matching Russian steppes-style hat, was wild and it stopped traffic in New York. Since it was the same streaky gray as my hair at that time, you couldn't tell where the outfit ended and I began.

As far as shopping's concerned, I'm a hopeless romantic. I buy things because I fall in love with them. I never buy anything because it's valuable. I have to get a physical reaction, a *coup de foudre*. I never plan what I need for each season. Eventually it all comes together. I enjoy the thrill of the chase, the discovery and the endless search. In another creation I was, perhaps, a hunter-gatherer.

My so-called "collection" is my wardrobe. I've been approximately the same size since high school. While my waistline hasn't expanded, my closet has. I just buy what I like and my tastes are quite catholic — haute couture to street fashion, Zen simple or madly baroque, ethnic or contemporary, serious or amusing. The *process* of putting things together is what it's all about.

I've also designed many things for myself — shoes, boots, bags, belts, jewelry, you name it. I never thought of doing it for others, especially not for people I wanted to keep as friends. Most women have a very specific image of themselves, and woe to anyone meddling with that.

One of the most stylish parades I've ever seen happened on a good spring Sunday afternoon in Harlem: everything from the swaggering youth in their vintage zoot suits or oversized rappy snappy Hilfigers to the resplendent retired ladies' maids on their way to church, wearing their madams' cast-off finery and extravagant headgear at a rakish angle.

Native Americans have great style as well, their gleaming copper skin a perfect foil for all that turquoise and silver, tons of it at a time. Or the Tibetan ladies, dressed to go out, piled high with bangles and beads and ear-dress.

Post-World War Two Europe was also a wonderful classroom for me. Style made up for the lack of many material things ("it ain't what you do, it's the way that you do it"). A motheaten silver fox scarf flung across "whatever" made an ordinary night on the town a stellar occasion. One never saw this more exquisitely illustrated than on the postwar streets of Naples (think Sophia Loren and Marcello Mastroianni). Even the hooker, all tarted up on the corner with her torn nylons, was *magnifica*. And so was the elderly beggar, elegant as could be, in his well-tailored, tattered morning suit, with his faded *boutonnière*. Such incredible pizzazz! My favorites, however, were the little boys, no more than nine years old, who served at the neighborhood coffee bars. They had large black-olive eyes and heavy crisp white cotton aprons down

Color, clothes, and Carl — a posse of my passions — surround me on our terrace in Capri, for many years the epicenter of our Mediterranean meanderings.

to the floor. When they turned round you observed their little backsides covered in teeny weeny short black shorts, their scrawny legs dangling down. Adorable! They're the reason I took to drinking espresso; I never drank a drop of coffee before that.

While of course we would all rather stay young, I say don't fret too much about the advent of old age. The alternative is most unpleasant. A few wrinkles won't do you in, and, while I don't approve, if they do there's always Botox. But better heed the warning that Coco Chanel supposedly gave: nothing makes a woman look so old as desperately trying to look young. The other big plus about aging is that you need no longer worry about how you look in a bikini. That in itself, to me, is worth at least ten summers.

Digging up my "stylish" unconscious has been a hoot. I've played the imaginary dual role of patient and shrink, leaping from chair to couch in a valiant effort to dredge up buried bits of my infamous fashion history, so inextricably intertwined with my Real Life. What fun to drag out these memories with a couple of single malt whiskies some dank dark evening round about midnight.…

Like arriving at the Danieli the first time Carl and I went to Venice and finding our suite loaded with flowers, as if a mafioso were being laid out. "What's this?" I gasped. It turned out that Roberta di Camerino, who made all those wonderful velvet handbags, had sent them to thank us because we'd been instrumental in jumpstarting the renaissance of the Italian fabric industry after the war. I invited her to come by for a drink. When we met, she asked, "Do you like clothes?" "Does a drunk like booze?" I replied. She recommended a couturier contessa to me, who made beautiful dresses for the "fiori di Venezia" as well as for the wife of Stanley Marcus, the retailing guru of Neiman Marcus. The next day I managed to find her palazzo but the contessa insisted she would only work with her own fabrics. As I was halfway out the door, she reconsidered and suggested I bring some of mine over. When she saw what I hauled back from the mill, she flipped out. From then on she made a number of things for me, including an incredible woven velvet tiger outfit [see p. 45]..... The Neapolitan afternoon at the

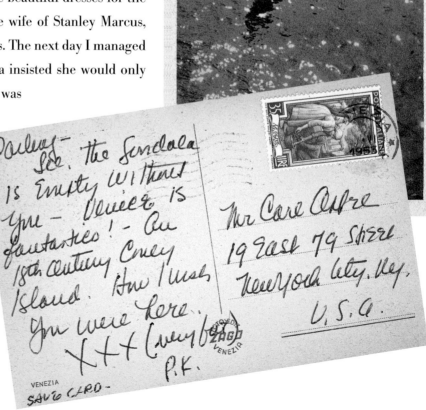

fabbrica of Mario Valentino where I first met Roger Vivier. The day was so so hot and he was so so cool he made me freeze, unable to express to him my reverence for his talent and his taste; how the very first thing I did upon arrival in Paris was to truck over to rue François 1er and worship at his shop window.… Climbing seven or eight flights of winding, wobbly, high-ceilinged stairs to the Parisian *atelier* of Mme. Gripoix, then swooning over her trays and trays of *faux bijoux extraordinaires*. I have yet to decide whether it was the rigors of the climb or the dazzle of the "gems" that most dizzied me.… At eighteen, that summer at the shore, where a new fashion-model friend taught me a trick of her trade — how to cook a spoonful of black mustache wax over a flame and hurriedly bead it onto my eyelashes (then long and lush). We thought the look sinfully wicked and *très très* sexy, and we *did* pre-date Miss Piggy!... The young man at a party who elatedly approved my great clunk of a faux metal bracelet. "Brava! Brava!" said he, "How Coco!" Once home I awakened

I shopped … he dropped. Carl, my private paparazzo, has always given me my space—especially in the closet

Mama excitedly with: "Can you imagine? I just met a boy who knows about Chanel!"... Browsing through the bazaars in Istanbul, Tunis, and Marrakesh, back then still laden with really spectacular treasure, and the little men in dhotis who always weighed the old silver chains and bangles and belt buckles in order to determine a price one could then haggle over.… Waiting for eight fashion seasons (four normal years), in the hope that a *manteau merveilleux* would get a further momentous markdown.… Jumping for joy when James Galanos agreed to design an ensemble for a very special charity luncheon, on the condition he work solely with my Old World Weavers fabrics. After the catwalk the finished product [see p. 123] fell blissfully into my grubby paws....

But enough about the past. I'm all for the future. You may ask, what is this octogenarian muse, this geriatric starlet, buying now? While I'm still ready to rumble round Ralph Rucci's resplendent regalia, or bedeck myself in beauteous Bill Blass by the brilliant Michael Vollbracht, or flip for my fabulous Ferré, or go-go with Gaultier, I'm buying jeans. They were one of my earliest pioneering statements and I adore them still. They're a canvas for creativity — wonderful with sables or sweats. Wear them to mow the lawn or disco till dawn. Bead them, tear them, tie-dye or embroider; they can be jeweled, flowered or furred; street fashion to haute couture. They can democratize even a Republican! Jeans, indeedy. What else would you suggest for the world's oldest living teenager?!

"Most people say
take one off;
    I say add one on"

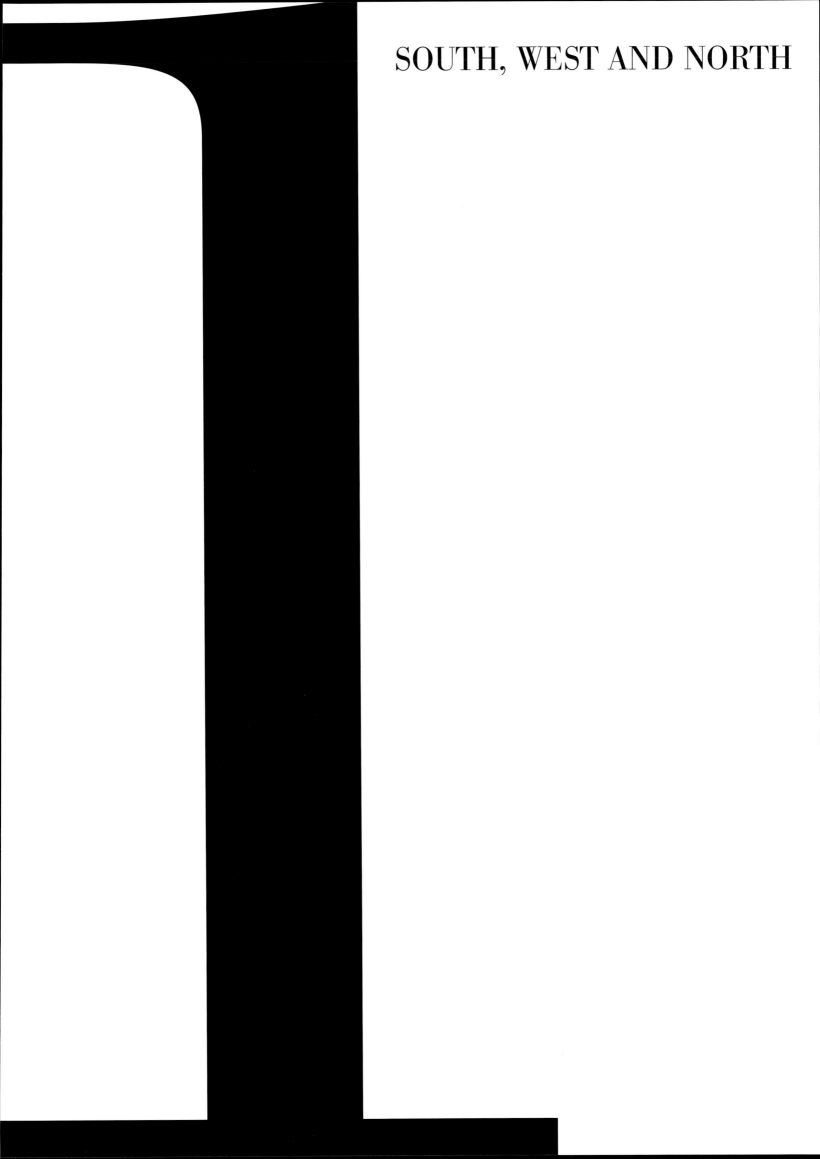

SOUTH, WEST AND NORTH

44

Necklace
South Seas, late 19th century
Seashell, coral, and cord

Textile
Leopard design hand-woven silk velvet on
linen warp upholstery fabric (Old World
Weavers)

45

**Travel ensemble, with matching duffel bag
and boots**
Iris Barrel Apfel by Contessa Adriana Biglia,
circa 1965
Tiger design hand-woven silk velvet on linen
warp upholstery fabric (Old World Weavers)

Bracelet
American, 1980s
Mah-jongg tiles, scorpions in Lucite and
black acrylic, elastic

46

left **Coat**
Nina Ricci haute couture by Gérard Pipart,
circa 1984
Brown leather with smocking and applied
oval silver studs

Boots
Italian, circa 1980
Brown leather

right **Tunic dress**
Oscar de la Renta, circa 1995
Brown wool and alpaca pile

"Turtle" brooch
Iradj Moini, circa 1990
Citrines, rhinestones, and metal

Necklace
Indian, late 19th century
Silver chain

Bracelets and bangles
Unknown, late 20th century
Acrylic faux amber

Tibetan, late 19th century
Silver and amber

Indian, early 20th century
Silver

Indian, 1980s
Colored rhinestones and metal

Boots
Manolo Blahnik for Ralph Rucci couture,
2004
Gold silk damask upholstery fabric (Old
World Weavers) and silk grosgrain ribbon

47

left **Turtleneck sweater**
American, circa 2002
Black wool knit

Cuirass
Gianfranco Ferré, 2002
Hand-forged metal

Trousers
Replay, circa 2002
Black synthetic leather

Spiral earring
Unknown, late 1960s
Chrome-plated metal

Boots
Ralph Lauren, late 1990s
Black leather

right **Vestment**
French, late 19th century
Black silk velvet with gold and silver metallic
thread embroidery and gold woven silk lining

Trousers
American, early 1970s
Black cotton velvet

Necklace
Italian, mid-20th century
Venetian glass with gilt tassel

Shoes
Charles Jourdan, circa 1987
Black cotton velour and gold metallic leather

48

Necklace
Unknown, circa 1940
Silver, turquoise, onyx, and bear claws

Pillow
Black velvet with American Indian motif
glass bead embroidery

49

Jacket
Lanvin haute couture by Jules-François
Crahay, circa 1989
Pink wool

Trousers
American, circa 1990
Black wool broadcloth

Necklaces
Indigenous American (Pueblo and Navajo
peoples), 1930s–1950s
Silver and turquoise

Cuff bracelets
Indigenous American, early 1970s
Silver, turquoise, and black and white
leather, with Kennedy silver dollar

Belt
Indigenous American (Navajo peoples),
1940s
Silver, turquoise, and leather

50

Cape
Norman Norell, circa 1959
Pink and orange mohair, with orange crochet
floss domed buttons

Turtleneck sweater
American, late 20th century
Orange wool knit

Bangles
Unknown, 1970s
Amber resin

51

Bangles
American, 1920s–1940s
Bakelite

Necklace
American, 1930s
"Marblette" Bakelite sample chips

52

top **Pendant**
Indian, early 20th century
Silver and turquoise

center left **Cuff bracelet**
Indigenous American (Navajo peoples),
1960s
Silver and turquoise

center **Ring**
Afghan, circa 1970s
Silver, etched glass, and turquoise

center right **Ring**
Tibetan, early 20th century
Silver, amber, coral, and turquoise

bottom **Cuff bracelet**
Indigenous American (Navajo peoples), 1940s
Silver and turquoise

53

Jumpsuit
Geoffrey Beene, 1992/93
Orange wool jersey

Shawl
English, late 20th century
Orange cashmere

"Scorpion" brooch
Indigenous American, 1980s
Silver and turquoise

Belt
Indigenous American, 1980s
Silver and turquoise

Cuff bracelet
Italian, 1970s
Turquoise ceramic and silver plate

54

Art Deco belt
Indigenous American (Zuni peoples), circa 1935
Silver, turquoise, coral, onyx, mother of pearl, and shell

"Needlepoint work" cuff bracelet
Indigenous American (Zuni peoples), 1960s
Silver and turquoise

Taos drum
American, 20th century
Wood and hide

55

from top **Belts**
Hungarian, mid-20th century
Leather and early 20th-century glass bead embroidery

American, circa 1972
Brass and steel ammunition bullets

André Courrèges, circa 1966
Brass

Central Asian, late 19th century
Silver, turquoise, and glass

right Transylvanian, late 19th century
Wool, leather, brass, silver, and glass

56

Cape
Indigenous American (Haida peoples), late 20th century
Black and red appliqué wool with abalone buttons and white wool fringe

Trousers
Krizia, circa 2000
Black crocodile stamped leather

Boots
Italian, circa 1981
Red suede

57

Jacket
Bill Blass, 1984
White, red, green, and navy wool

Dance skirt
Indigenous American (Hopi peoples), circa 2000
White cotton canvas and red suede, with metal bell fringe

Neck scarf
American, 1990s
Black Tibetan lamb

Necklace
American, 1930s
Black and red Bakelite beads

Boots
Italian, circa 1972
Black goat fur

58

left **Coat**
Stella Forest, circa 2003
Pieced and clipped silver fox

Belt
African, late 20th century
Brown linen wall hanging with black, brown, white, red, and blue seed bead and cowry shell embroidery

Coolie hat
Ralph Rucci couture, 2005
Black silk gros de longres

Boots
Etro, circa 2003
Red wool with red, black, and white paillette and bead embroidery

right **Coat**
J. Mendel, 1984
White and brown lynx-spotted fox fur

Boots
European, circa 1990
Black leather and natural cowhide

59

Jumpsuit
Jean Paul Gaultier, 1991/92
Gray and white wool blend shadow check twill with white wool/faux fur trim

Hat
American, circa 1965
Brown Persian lamb

Hat pin
South American, 1940s
Metal, colored stones, and tin fish

Neck square
American, late 20th century
Paisley printed sheer wool

Belt
Iris Barrel Apfel, 1960s
Composite braided leather with South American tin fish

60

Coat
Fendi by Karl Lagerfeld, circa 1982
Tortoise-dyed Mongolian lamb and pieced squirrel

61

Poncho
Italian, 1980s
Red Persian lamb and rabbit fur pile with brown leather lining

Trousers
Christian Dior haute couture, circa 2002
Ivory cotton twill with wolf fur trim

Belt
Unknown (tribal), mid-20th century
Red cotton velvet with applied shells

Shoes
French, circa 1994
Ponyskin and black rubber

"I'm not a lady
who lunches"

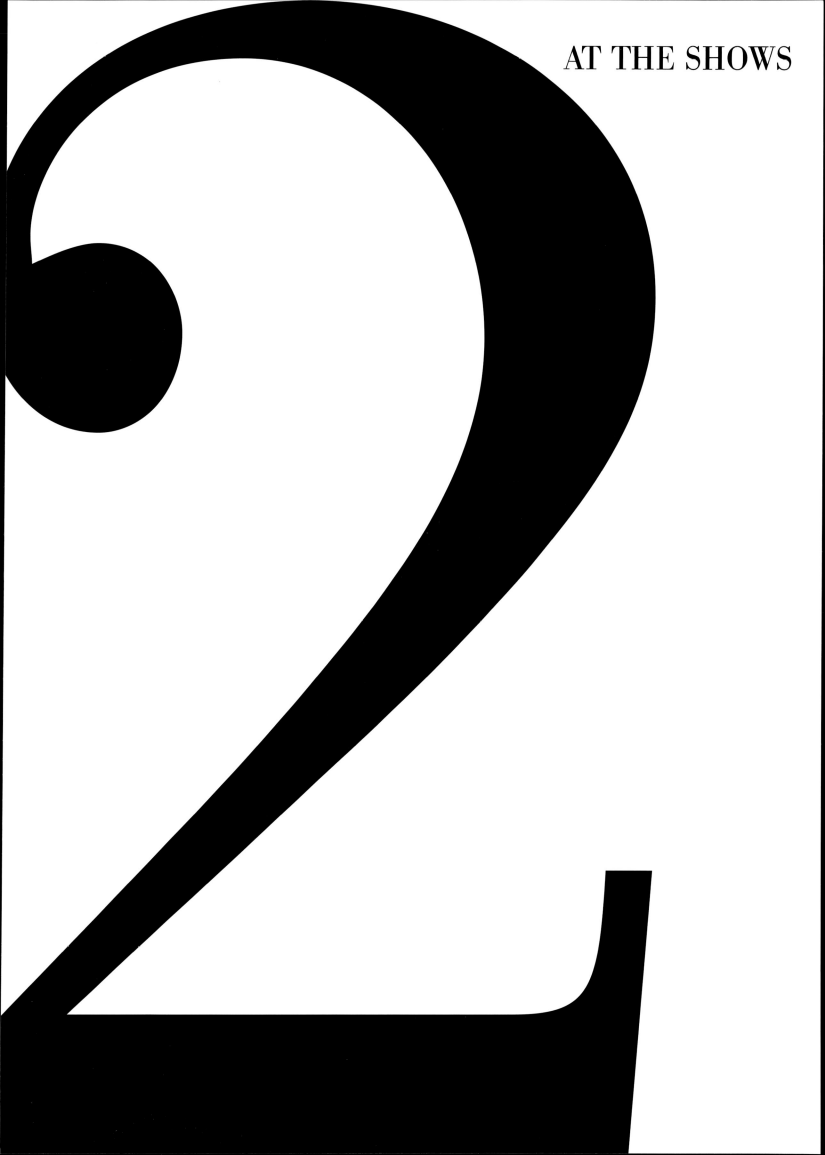

66

Cuff bracelets
Valentino, circa 1990
Acrylic and rhinestones

"Dragonfly" brooch
Giorgio Armani, circa 2003
Crocodile-embossed black leather, acrylic,
and rhinestones

Earring
American (flea-market find), 1970s
Spent flashbulb and metal

67

Jacket
Christian Dior haute couture by Gianfranco
Ferré, circa 1986
Black and white Mongolian lamb with black
and white ostrich feathers

Trousers
Gianfranco Ferré, circa 1998
Black and white Glen plaid wool

Necklace and bracelets
Monies, circa 1999
Wood and leather

Shoes
Stuart Weitzman, circa 1994
Black and white pieced grosgrain

68

Coat
Nina Ricci haute couture by Gérard Pipart,
circa 1984
Gray, black, and white mohair

Textile [at neck]
Pink silk

Necklaces and bracelet
Angela Caputi Giugiù, late 1990s
Black and gray acrylic

Boots
Iris Barrel Apfel by Canfora, circa 1978
Gray wool and pink leather

69

Tunic
Gianfranco Ferré, circa 1994
Brown nutria and wool knit

Trousers
Unknown, circa 1990s
Tweed-effect brown and gray wool with gold
thread; self-fabric pile crochet cuffs

Necklaces
European, late 1970s
Baltic amber and silver

Bangles
Various, 20th century
Wood, amber, and acrylic

Ring
European, circa 1990
Baltic amber and wood

70

Coat
Nina Ricci haute couture by Gérard Pipart,
circa 1979
Gray, beige, and ivory striped wool with
silver fox fur cuffs

Muff
American, late 20th century
Silver fox fur

Scarf
American, mid-20th century
Silver fox fur and gray silk satin

71

Coat
Christian Dior haute couture by Gianfranco
Ferré, circa 1996
Black and white plaid silk jacquard with
silver fox fur trim

Dog collar necklace
Angela Caputi Giugiù, 1990s
Black acrylic, rhinestones, and metal

"Star" brooch
Nina Ricci haute couture, circa 1987
Black acrylic, rhinestones, and metal

Shoes
Guido Pasquali, circa 1986
Black suede, white leather, and white wood
ball heels

72

Cape
Nepalese, 1970s
Ivory wool knit with pile fringe and self-
fabric pompons

Skirt
Gianfranco Ferré, 1990s
Black and beige buffalo checked wool

Necklaces
Indian, early 20th century
Silver and snail shells

Monies, circa 1999
Bone chips

Chinese, circa 2003
Carved bone

Tibetan, circa 1970
Carved bone

Bangles
Indian, early 20th century
Ivory and wood

Boots
American, circa 1994
Black synthetic suede cloth

73

Coat
Carlo Ferrini, circa 1983
White, black, and gray wool looped pile knit

Necklaces
Monies, circa 1990
Wood and waxed black cotton cord

Bangle
Monies, circa 1995
Wood

Shoes
Manolo Blahnik, 1992
Black leather and gray lizard skin

74

Purse
American (flea-market find), circa 2000
Painted metal and black leather

75

Jacket
Geoffrey Beene, 1994/95
Black and white bouclé wool twill with stem-
stitch black and white wool and black bugle
bead trapunto embroidery

Trousers
Donna Karan, circa 1992
Black and white flecked wool Donegal tweed

Necklaces
English, 1960s
Black and clear crystal and rhinestones

Cuff bracelets
European, 1960s
Black acrylic, rhinestones, and metal

Boots
Delman, circa 2000
Black and white wool Donegal tweed

76

Coat
Jean-Louis Scherrer haute couture,
circa 1980
Ivory and black wool

Necklace
French, circa 1980
Pearlized papier mâché, black acrylic,
and rhinestones

77

Coat
Norman Norell, circa 1962
Ivory and black wool

Earring and bracelet
American, 2004
Black and white wood beads and black
elastic hair ties

Ring
Monies, circa 2001
Wood and bone

Shoes
Kate Spade, circa 1999
Black silk satin with white leather trim

78

Shirtdress
Chado Ralph Rucci, 2004
Ivory, brown, and black "Rorschach Test"
printed cotton broadcloth

Necklaces
Unknown, circa 2000
Wood and brown elastic cord

Iris Barrel Apfel, circa 1965
Composite 20th-century Indian ivory,
wood, and metal "bird" perfume bottle
with antique Indian silver chain

Cuff bracelets
Caribbean, 1990s
Coconut shell

79

Tunic
Krizia, circa 1990
White leather with black spatter print

Necklace
Iris Barrel Apfel, circa 2003
Composite black and white wood beads

Cuff bracelet
Monies, circa 2000
Exotic wood

Boots
Italian, circa 1980
Black leather

80

Shirt
Gianfranco Ferré, circa 1995
White net with ivory cotton over-embroidery
and ivory satin collar

Trousers
Rifat Ozbek, circa 1992
Black pinstriped silk velvet with faux abalone
button decoration

"Salamander" brooches
European, 1920s
Black glass, rhinestones, and metal

Shoes
Giorgio Armani, circa 2003
Black silk satin with white beading

81

Ensemble
Mila Schön, circa 1967
Black crocodile-embossed patent leather
with black mink fur trim

Necklace
Belgian, circa 2000
Black leather, faux horn, and tan leather
tasseled curtain tieback

Bangles
Monies, circa 1995
Wood

Shoes
Philippe Model, circa 1996
Mustard suede

82

Tunic
Chado Ralph Rucci, 1999
Beige double-faced grain de poudre wool

Trousers
Gianfranco Ferré, circa 1996
Bronze silk satin

Necklace
Iris Barrel Apfel, circa 2002
Composite early 20th-century European
articulated wood and metal hands with late
19th-century South American wood rosary
beads

Bangles
Unknown, 1990s
Carved faux amber

Tibetan, early 20th century
Amber and silver

American, 1980s
Wood

Shoes
Chanel by Karl Lagerfeld, circa 1998
Pewter and gold silk satin with clear acrylic
wedge heels

83

Necklace
Lanvin, early 1980s
Gilded papier mâché, acrylic beads,
and satin ribbon

Round pillow
Silk damask upholstery fabric (Old World
Weavers)

Textile
Lelièvre silk damask upholstery fabric
(Old World Weavers)

"In the right tonality
     I never met a color
I didn't like"

3

88

Evening dress
Lanvin haute couture by Jules-François
Crahay, circa 1985
Gold, brown, and pewter silk faille

Necklaces
Tibetan, early 20th century
Silver, amber, coral, and turquoise

Cuff bracelets
Bhutanese, late 19th century
Silver and amber

Tibetan, late 19th century
Silver, amber, coral, and turquoise

89

Cuff bracelets
Tibetan, early 20th century
Silver, amber, coral, and turquoise

Tibetan, late 19th century
Silver, turquoise, and amber

Tibetan, late 19th century
Silver, coral, and turquoise

Tibetan, late 19th century
Silver, turquoise, and amber

Tibetan, early 20th century
Silver, gold, turquoise, and coral

Tibetan, early 20th century
Silver, coral, and turquoise

90

Brooch
Gripoix, circa 1970
Commissioned in antique lacquered metal
and rhinestones by Iris Barrel Apfel

Textile
Lelièvre silk damask upholstery fabric (Old
World Weavers)

91

Evening dress
Lanvin haute couture by Jules-François
Crahay, circa 1983
Red violet and blue violet *changeant* faille
with red facing

Necklace
Apex Art, circa 1968
Glass, rhinestones, and metal

Ring
Italian, 20th century
Amethyst, fire opal, and gold

Shoes
Gianfranco Ferré, circa 1990
Red suede with gold metal ball trim

92

Evening coat
Lanvin haute couture by Jules-François
Crahay, circa 1983
Iridescent purple and blue silk blend
ottoman

Necklace
Iris Barrel Apfel, 2005
Composite American gilded wood beads
and leather with African (Fulani) hammered
gold earrings

Shoes
American, circa 1999
Hand-stenciled multicolored leather

93

Evening dress
James Galanos, 1989
Midnight blue silk georgette bodice with
matching silk crêpe skirt

Bracelets
French, late 1960s
Metal, rhinestones, and faux pearls

Shoes
Salvatore Ferragamo, circa 1964
Platinum metallic leather and silver painted
wood

94

Evening coat
Koos van den Akker, 1983
Crushed black cotton velvet with multicolored
metallic appliqués and gilt braid trim

Mask
Venetian, late 20th century
Cloth, paper, and feathers

95

Evening jumpsuit and bolero
Jean-Louis Scherrer haute couture, circa 1975
Blue silk blend damask with silver lamé
appliqués, and silver bugle bead,
multicolored chenille, and black, pink, and
blue paillette embroidery

Head ornament
American (flea-market find), mid-20th
century
Multicolored rhinestone and lacquered
metal bow brooch

96

Evening coat
Emanuel Ungaro haute couture, circa 1984
Ribbons of layered purple, blue, and yellow
tulle applied over red violet satin

Trousers
Moschino, 2002
Pink, purple, and fuchsia metallic leather

Necklaces
Unknown
Rhinestones, pink beads, and silk-covered
beads

Bracelets
Unknown, late 20th century
Multicolored rhinestones, paillettes, and
metal

Necklace [in hand]
Portuguese, circa 1975
Silver, amethyst, and pearls

Shoes
Italian, circa 1987
Pink metallic leather

97

Evening dress
Nina Ricci haute couture by Gérard Pipart,
circa 1986
Red, gold, fuchsia, and black floral silk chiné
with red, black, and topaz rhinestone buttons

Earrings
American, late 1960s
Gilt metal ball chain and gold Mylar

Shoes
Manolo Blahnik, circa 1997
Red silk satin

98

Evening coat
Nina Ricci haute couture by Jules-François
Crahay, circa 1959
Pistachio silk duchesse satin with green
rhinestone buttons

Stole
American, 1980s
Red dyed fox fur

Shoes
Christian Lacroix, circa 1991
Red silk satin with gold metallic leather
appliqués

99

left **Coat**
Nina Ricci haute couture by Gérard Pipart,
late 1970s
Shocking pink marabou feathers

Trousers
Dolce & Gabbana, circa 2000
Purple, shocking pink, and blue paisley silk
jacquard with multicolored rhinestone, gold
paillette and gold bead embroidery

Earring
Unknown, late 1960s
Turquoise, green and beige resin,
rhinestones, and metal

Necklace
Apex Art, late 1960s
Turquoise glass, rhinestones, and metal

Shoes
British, 1990s
Pink silk satin

right **Coat**
André Laug haute couture, late 1970s
Dark burgundy marabou feathers

Trousers
Chado Ralph Rucci, 2001/2
Oxblood wool barathea

Shawl
Indian (Kashmiri), late 20th century
Multicolored cashmere and silk with floral
embroidery

Necklace
Iris Barrel Apfel, 2005
Composite purple crystal beads and
rhinestones with metal and enamel
Chinese fish

Cuff bracelet
Indian, circa 2003
Painted wood with glass inserts

Shoes
Iris Barrel Apfel by Canfora, mid-1960s
Burgundy silk satin

100

"Parrot" brooch
Iradj Moini, circa 1990
Pink, blue, and green glass with rhinestones
and metal

Textile
Pink faux fur

101

Coat
Emanuel Ungaro, circa 2000
Ombré pink and light pink striped clipped
rabbit fur with skin side inside

Trousers
Emanuel Ungaro, circa 1999
Dark pink velvet with resist-printed light
pink polka dots

"Star" brooch
American, circa 1983
Pink acrylic and blue rhinestones

Shoes
Kate Spade, circa 2002
Pink silk satin

102

Coat
Jean-Louis Scherrer haute couture, late
1990s
Black and gold-tipped duck feathers

Trousers
Roberto Cavalli, circa 2002
Leopard-printed cotton blend laminated
with clear sequin effect

Necklaces
French, 1930s
Gilt metal and rhinestone beads

Monies, 2005
Tea-stained bone

Apex Art, 1950s
Acrylic, glass, rhinestones, and metal

103

left **Jacket**
Jean-Louis Scherrer haute couture, 1990/91
Black, gray, orange and red rooster, duck
and fowl feathers

Carnival mask [also on chair]
Venetian, late 20th century
Molded cloth-covered paper

Booted stockings
Unknown, early 1970s
Dark navy stretch satin

right **Jacket**
Nina Ricci haute couture by Gérard Pipart,
late 1970s
Purple, orange, red and green duck and
rooster feathers

Trousers
Moschino, 1997
Red slashed suede

Bangles
Indian, circa 2003
Multicolored rhinestones and metal

Shoes
Anne Klein, circa 1989
Pink silk satin with orange silk faille ribbons

"I was born with a Souk Sense"

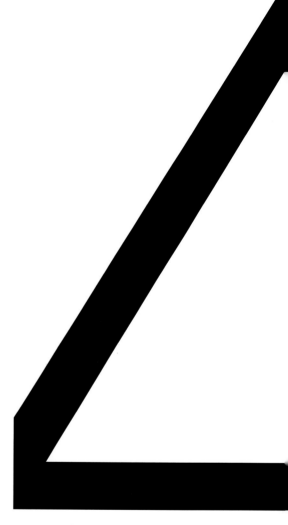

1

THIS IS A

**10-DAY
LOAN
SAMPLE**

**PLEASE
DO NOT
CUT**

THANK YOU FOR
YOUR COOPERATION!

OLD WORLD WEAVERS
Fabric Division of Stark Carpet Corp.

108

Headdress
Indian (Ladakh), late 19th century
Wool, amber, coral, turquoise, and silver

Scarf
Indian embroidered silk upholstery fabric
sample (Old World Weavers)

Neck ornament
Indian (Ladakh), early 20th century
Wool, silver, amber, coral, turquoise, and
wood

Necklaces
Chinese, late 19th century
Silver and coral

Iris Barrel Apfel, circa 2005
Composite late 19th-century Tibetan silver,
amber and coral frogs with amber, coral and
silver beads

109

Jacket
Ralph Rucci Chado haute couture, circa
2003
Dark brown, light brown, and black
horsehair (Old World Weavers)

Trousers
Oscar de la Renta, circa 2000
Brown silk faille

Brooch, necklaces, and bracelets
Angela Caputi Giugiù, circa 1990
Black and coral acrylic and rhinestones

Bangles
Italian, 1980s
Faux coral

110

Vest
Gianfranco Ferré, circa 1993
Multicolored paisley-printed silk twill with
multicolored wood seed bead, faux abalone,
ivory stone, and multicolored paillette
embroidery

Shirt
Italian, circa 1997
Purple silk

Skirt
Joie, circa 2004
Black cotton canvas

Cuff bracelets
American, 1970s
Ivory plastic

Necklaces
Monies, circa 2003
White bone chips and black waxed cotton
cord

Boots
Italian, circa 1987
Red suede

111

Jacket
Oscar de la Renta, circa 2000
Multicolored patchwork of silk faille, silk
damask, and cotton velvet with multicolored
silk and gold filé thread and gold metal
paillette embroidery

Necklaces
Angela Caputi Giugiù, circa 2001
Acrylic and metal

Boots
Kenzo, circa 1990
Taupe suede

112

"Tali" necklace
Southern Indian (Chettiar woman's 50th
wedding anniversary necklace), 19th century
Gold, with black silk cord

113

Tunic
Tunisian (wedding garment), early 20th
century
Red and black wool gauze with gold paillette,
coiled thread, and hammered metal
embroidery, green and gold braided piping,
and blue silk and metallic filé trapunto

Necklaces
Givenchy, 1970s
Black, red, and gray silk passementerie with
rhinestones

Necklaces and bracelet
Monies, circa 2003
Gilded wood

114

Coat
British (flea-market find)
Antique British paisley wool shawls

Carrying case
Tibetan, late 19th century
Silver, copper, amber, coral, and turquoise,
with fabric and leather

Purse
French, late 19th century
Paisley wool shawl and hammered silver
amalgam

Brooch
Turkish, early 20th century
Converted metal belt buckle with turquoise
and amber glass

Necklaces
American (flea-market find), 2003
Mahogany beads

Boots
Iris Barrel Apfel by Canfora, 1970s
Antique paisley wool shawls and leather

115

left **Shawl**
Indian (Rajasthani), mid-20th century
Resist-dyed magenta wool with multicolored
cotton and mirror embroidery

Skirt and trousers
Escada, circa 1995
Red, orange, black, and gold lamé paisley-
patterned brocade

Chest ornament
Afghan, early 20th century
Burgundy, ivory and brown printed cotton,
silver, and cornelian

Cuff bracelet
Afghan, early 20th century
Silver and cornelian

Shoes
Etro, 1990s
Paisley cotton jacquard, turquoise cotton
velvet, and multicolored beading

right **Jacket**
European (flea-market find)
Olive, beige, mustard, and red paisley
patterned wool twill with red and white
seed bead embroidery

Trousers
European, circa 1980
Burgundy and brown leather, hand-stained
by Karl Springer

Necklace
Chinese Minority, late 19th century
Silver

Belt
Central Asian, late 19th century
Metal

Cuff bracelets
Indian, late 19th century
Silver

Boots
Romeo Gigli, circa 1989
Cinnabar cotton poplin

116

Jacket
Christian Dior haute fourrure by John
Galliano, circa 2000
Black and white Persian lamb with rainbow-
colored tulle appliqué, quilted in chevron
pattern

Trousers
Gianfranco Ferré, circa 1999
Jacquard matelassé of tobacco-brown ground
with multicolored silk flowers

Necklaces
Angela Caputi Giugiù, circa 2000
Black and amber acrylic and silk cord

European, 1970s
Black glass and rhinestones

Bib necklace
European, circa 1999
Baltic amber and crocheted thread

Bangles
Unknown, 1980s
Amber glass and acrylic

Monies, 1980s
Faux amber

Shoes
Salvatore Ferragamo, late 20th century
Stamped cinnabar suede

117

left **Cape**
Nina Ricci haute couture by Gérard Pipart,
circa 1991
Multicolored paisley-patterned cashmere and
multicolored paisley-printed silk damask

Necklace
Afghan, late 19th century
Silver and cornelian

Boots
Susan Bennis/Warren Edwards, circa 1988
Aubergine suede

right **Sweater**
French, circa 1982
Rhubarb cashmere and angora knit

Trousers
Lanvin haute couture by Jules-François
Crahay, circa 1983
Pink and rose gold crinkled lamé

Hat
American, circa 1987
Burgundy and black Mongolian lamb

Brooch
Turkish, early 20th century
Converted decorative ornament of metal with
amber and turquoise glass

Cuff bracelet
Colombian, 1970s
Gilt metal

Bangles
American, late 20th century
Plastic

Shoes
Charles Jourdan, circa 1991
Gold metallic leather

118

left **Jacket**
Christian Dior haute couture by John
Galliano, circa 2000
Pieced Mongolian and Chinese embroidered
chartreuse silk on metallic purple and gold
silk brocade, applied metal charms, and
amber wool fringe trim

Trousers
Yves Saint Laurent, circa 1989
Green floral silk cloqué

Chest ornament
Chinese, Qing Dynasty
Multicolored enameled silver

Necklace
Chinese, Qing Dynasty
Cloisonné beads

Shoes
Emanuel Ungaro, circa 1990
Blue lizard-embossed leather, with red
paillette and green seed bead floral
embroidery

right **Cocoon wrap**
Lanvin haute couture by Jules-François
Crahay, circa 1983
Emerald green and royal blue *changeant*
silk dupioni taffeta

Necklace
Indigenous American (Navajo peoples),
circa 1930s
Silver and turquoise

Cuff bracelet
South Pacific Islands, early 20th century
Silver

Shoes
Romeo Gigli, late 1980s
Emerald and olive green *changeant* silk
taffeta

119

left **Coat**
Afghan, early 20th century
Green wool with burgundy wool stem-stitch
embroidery, salmon herringbone wool inset
with multicolored silk thread embroidery,
silver metal coin and charms with turquoise
and amber insets

Necklaces
Italian, mid-20th century
Faux coral beads with bone and brass

Shoes
American, early 1990s
Dark green suede

right **Coat**
Afghan, 20th century
Green linen/wool blend with applied silver
metal coins and charms inset with turquoise
and cornelian, and red and black wool
fringe trim

Necklaces
American, 2005
Synthetic pebbles

American (flea-market find)
Exotic wood beads

Boots
Italian, circa 1987
Green leather and multicolored cotton thread
embroidery

120

"Butterfly" brooch
French, circa 1910
Metal, blue glass, and rhinestone converted
belt buckle

Antique traveling case
Chinese, 19th century
Hand-painted vellum

121

Twin sweater set
Krizia, 1980s
Cornelian angora wool knit

Skirt
Chinese, Qing Dynasty
Yellow silk damask with multicolored silk
brocade, blue silk satin, and multicolored silk
and filé thread embroidery

Mandarin necklace
Chinese, Qing Dynasty
Silk cord, cornelian, jade, and metal

Cuff bracelet
European, circa 1989
Amber resin and rhinestones

Boots
Iris Barrel Apfel by Canfora, circa 1980
Peach leather

Birdcages
Chinese, 1950s
Bamboo, porcelain, and metal

122

Jacket
Roberto Cavalli, circa 2002
Light blue cotton denim with multicolored
floral embroidery and white cotton twill
tape appliqué

Jeans
American, circa 1990
Light indigo cotton denim

Clip
Unknown, 1930s
Multicolored glass, rhinestones, and metal

Purse
Unknown, circa 2000
Pink Mongolian lamb and gold metal

123

Evening ensemble
James Galanos, circa 1969
Spolinato coat of handwoven multicolored
wool flowers on natural linen (Old World
Weavers), hammered metal buttons, and
sable fur trim with antique burnt orange
satin-backed silk dupioni taffeta lining,
and matching sleeveless dress

Necklaces and bracelets
Monies, circa 2004
Horn and black cord

Shoes
Unknown, circa 1969
Purple silk velvet and pheasant feathers

124

"Harem" jewelry
Turkish, last quarter 19th century

top left "Bird" brooch
Gold, enamel, and diamonds

top right "Butterfly" brooch
Gold, enamel, and diamonds

bottom left "Bees" brooch
Gold, enamel, gray pearl, and diamonds

bottom right "Flower spray" brooch
Gold, diamonds, and rubies

Pincushions
English, circa 1980s
Pieced 18th-century fabrics and
20th-century trims

125

Evening coat
Christian Dior haute fourrure by John
Galliano, circa 2001
Black mountain goat fur-lined ivory silk
taffeta, embroidered in the manner of an
18th-century gentleman's waistcoat, with
embroidered blue denim pockets

Jeans
American, 2000
Indigo cotton denim

Mask
Venetian, late 20th century
Molded cloth-covered paper

Earrings
American, circa 1990
Cotton denim, rhinestones, and metal

Bangles
Unknown (flea-market find), circa 1990
Multicolored rhinestones and beads

Boots
Iris Barrel Apfel by Canfora, 1970s
Black satin with black jet heels

126

"Moghul" earrings and necklace
Gripoix, circa 1960
Metal, faux pearls, blue and green glass,
and rhinestones

"Peacock feather" brooches
Gripoix, circa 1960
Custom-made replicas of 18th-century jewel
commissioned by Iris Barrel Apfel in metal,
blue and green glass, and rhinestones

127

Brooch [on ear]
Gripoix, circa 1960
Leaves of metal and red and green glass,
with faux pearls and rhinestones

Bib necklace
Gripoix, circa 1964
Metal, red and green glass, faux pearls,
and rhinestones

Pendant necklace
Turkish, late 19th century
Gold, enamel, pink jade, and diamonds

Necklace
Gripoix, circa 1958
Clusters of metal, red and green glass, faux
pearls, and rhinestones

Bracelet
Gripoix, circa 1960 [en suite with brooch]
Flower of metal and red and green glass,
with faux pearls and rhinestones

Textile
Gold silk damask upholstery fabric
(Old World Weavers)

128

Doge's hat
Venetian, 20th century
Molded damask-covered paper with
passementerie

"Harem" brooch
Turkish, last quarter 19th century
Plumes of gold and diamonds on red enamel

129

Ensemble
Iris Barrel Apfel (dressmaker unknown),
1958
Mauve and multicolored floral silk broché
upholstery fabric (Old World Weavers)

Necklaces
Gripoix, 1960s
Faux pearls, blue, red and green glass,
rhinestones, and metal

Bracelets
Chinese and European, 1960s
Multicolored rhinestones, gilt metal, and
faux pearls

Bangles
Alexis Bittar, circa 1992
Handcarved Lucite with oxidized sterling
silver

130

Evening dress and bolero
Geoffrey Beene, 1990/91
Green and orange polka dot silk taffeta dress,
with bodice of quilted orange silk twill and
black panne velvet; multicolored silk, silver
and gold metallic coin-embroidered black
silk gazar bolero

Necklaces
European, 1980s
Orange and black acrylic, rhinestones,
and metal

Unknown, 1970s
Colored glass, rhinestones, faux pearls, and
metal

"Blackamoor" brooch
Nardi, 1970s
Gold, baroque pearls, enamel, and diamonds

Bangles
Angela Caputi Giugiù, 1980s
Faux coral

Angela Caputi Giugiù, 1980s
Metallic-lined green resin

Bangles and bracelets
Unknown (flea-market finds)
Colored glass, rhinestones, faux pearls, and
metal

Shoes
American, circa 1992
Woven orange silk satin ribbons

131

"Blackamoor" brooch
Codognato, 19th century
Gold, enamel, coral and diamonds, set with
17th-century coral cameos

Textile
Lelièvre silk upholstery fabric (Old World
Weavers)

"Controlled baroque,
               that's me"

5

INTO THE NIGHT

155

138

Necklace
American, 1980s
Black and white plastic twist-link toy

Bangles
American, 1970s
Plastic and paper stuffed toy animal eyes

139

Coat
Christian Dior haute couture by Gianfranco
Ferré, circa 1995
White silk satin appliquéd with white cotton
floral pieces, over-embroidered with white
cotton and white silk thread

Necklaces and bracelets
Apex Art (flea-market find), 1950s
White glass, rhinestones, and metal

Mask
Venetian, late 20th century
White molded plastic

140

"Mermaid" dress
Norman Norell, 1964/65
Ivory silk organza with patinated silver
sequin and white ostrich feather embroidery

Shoes
Susan Bennis/Warren Edwards, 1990s
Gold metallic leather

141

Earrings
Apex Art (flea-market find), 1960s
Metal and rhinestones

Sautoir
Roger Jean-Pierre, circa 1960
Metal, smoky topaz glass, and rhinestones

Textile
Ombré bronze metallic synthetic curtain
fabric (Old World Weavers)

142

left **Cape and dress**
Simonetta alta moda, circa 1965
Coral silk twill cape; matching dress with
green chenille, rhinestone, seed bead, and
bugle bead floral embroidered bodice

Necklace
European, 1960s
Clear and green glass, rhinestones, and metal

Bracelets
European, 1980s
Green glass and metal

Bangle
Patricia von Muslin, circa 1980
Translucent Lucite

"Palm" brooch
Gripoix, circa 1978
Emerald green baguette rhinestones and
metal

Shoes
Spanish, circa 1987
Green silk satin with rhinestones

right **Cape**
Simonetta alta moda, circa 1965
Magenta silk organza

Necklaces
Monies, circa 2004
Transparent acrylic with silver flakes

Bangles
Alexis Bittar, circa 1992
Handcarved Lucite with sterling silver leaf

Unknown, 1980s
Shaped silver resin and rhinestones

Shoes
Moschino, circa 2000
Silver, gray, and white mohair bouclé with
silver leather trim and rhinestone and pearl
buckle

143

left **Evening coat**
Lanvin haute couture by Antonio del Castillo,
early 1950s
Vermilion silk twill

Bib necklace
Christian Lacroix, circa 1988
Gilt metal mesh, faux pearls, rhinestones,
and red and green glass beads

Bangles
Indian, late 20th century
Metallic plastic with colored glass

American, late 20th century
Metallic acrylic with rhinestones

Mules
Philippe Model, mid-1980s
Gold metallic leather with vermilion suede

center **Cape**
Pauline Trigère, late 1950s
Lacquer red silk velvet

Necklaces
Tibetan, mid-20th century
Coral and turquoise beads

Shoes
Iris Barrel Apfel by Canfora, circa 1985
Multicolored floral silk and linen blend
brocade

right **Evening dress and stole**
Norman Norell, circa 1963
Red and gold *changeant* silk taffeta, with
sable fur trim

Bracelets
Valentino, circa 1993
Lacquer red acrylic, rhinestones, and metal

Shoes
Christian Lacroix, circa 1987
Lacquer red suede with gold metallic thread
embroidery

144

left **"Baby Doll" dress**
Nina Ricci haute couture by Gérard Pipart,
circa 1968
Coral silk floral organza

Pendant brooch
Apex Art (flea-market find), circa 1960
Gilt metal, rhinestones, and faux pearls

Shoes
Iris Barrel Apfel by Canfora, circa 1985
Multicolored woven silk ribbons and silver
metallic leather

right **Evening coat and shawl**
Nina Ricci haute couture by Gérard Pipart,
circa 1967
Cerulean blue silk gazar

Necklace
Gripoix, 1970s
Metal with turquoise and red glass beads

Bangles
Chinese, early 20th century
Enameled silver

Boots
Iris Barrel Apfel by Canfora, late 1960s
Turquoise suede with antique multicolored
floral needlepoint trim

145

Evening coat
Norman Norell, circa 1962
White, fuschia, pink, and ombré purple and pink silk crêpe de chine anemones with applied raffia and pile pistils

Boots
Kenzo, circa 1990
Pink suede

146

Dress
James Galanos, circa 1968
Ivory silk satin ribbons

Purse [worn as necklace]
Giorgio Armani, circa 2003
Stingray leather, acrylic, and metal

147

Smoking
Norman Norell, circa 1969
Brown silk velvet and ivory silk satin

Necklace
American (flea-market find), 1980s
Glass, acrylic, rhinestones, and metal

Shoes
Walter Steiger, circa 1995
Brown silk satin

148

Evening jumpsuit
James Galanos, 1981/82
Over-embroidered black silk lace bodice with rhinestones, and gray on gray silk taffeta gingham pantaloons with brocaded gold and silver lamé floral sprigs

Earrings
American, circa 1967
Clear and black glass, gilt metal, and rhinestones

Shoes
Ralph Lauren, 1990s
Black silk satin with black suede ribbon appliqué

149

Necklace
Indian, late 19th century
Silver and black cotton ribbon ceremonial horse ornament

Ponytail
Horsehair sample for weaving upholstery fabric (Old World Weavers)

150

Dress
James Galanos, circa 1970s
Brown and beige giraffe-printed silk chiffon

Cuff bracelet
American, circa 1981
Wood, fabric, and rhinestones

Boots
Italian, circa 1990
Brown suede with leopard-printed gold lamé

151

Evening dress
James Galanos, 1970s
Silver lamé polka dot chiffon jacquard with black and rust medallion overprint, metallic bronze rope macramé, and gold seed bead tassels

Bamboo bangle [on ear]
Chinese, early 20th century
Black lacquer

Bangles
Monies, 1990s
Ebonized wood

American (flea-market find), 20th century
Amber resin

Magnifying glass
American, 20th century
Silver plate and glass

152

Cuff bracelets
Christian Dior by Gianfranco Ferré haute couture, circa 1995
Gilt metal

Chanel, circa 1989
Gilt metal, black leather, and faux pearls

Buddha hand
Unknown (flea-market find), late 19th century
Gilt metal

153

Evening coat
Antonio del Castillo haute couture, circa 1961
Gold lamé ribbon appliqué on gold Mylar with cluster embroidery of gold and silver paillettes, beads, and rhinestones

Necklaces
Tibetan, early 20th century
Amber, turquoise, and silver

Bracelets and bangles
Unknown, 1970s
Green glass and metal

Unknown, 1970s
Topaz glass and metal

American, mid-20th century
Topaz rhinestones and gilt metal

Cuff bracelet
Thierry Mugler, circa 1990
Gilt metal and topaz rhinestones

Gloves
American, circa 2000
Gilt Lycra

Booted trousers
Anne Klein, mid-1980s
Green stretch panné velvet and gold metallic leather

154

Bridal headdress
Chinese, Qing Dynasty
Kingfisher feathers, silver, seed pearls, coral, and multicolored stones

Shoulder purse
Chinese, Qing Dynasty
Pieced multicolored silk cloud-shaped collar fragments

155

Snake bracelet
Iradj Moini, circa 1990
Articulated metal, black and blue glass, and rhinestones

Apple
Golden Delicious hand-colored with red lipstick

158

overleaf **Necklace**
JingleGems, 1983–1985
Multicolored plastic charm belt

Acknowledgments

The vision of Harold Koda made the exhibition that sparked this book, and I thank him for his support and for his lucid introduction.

Iris Barrel Apfel was the rare subject who took the time and effort, not only to contribute a text, but to follow every step of the book's development, and her input has been invaluable in making it true to her spirit.

For some fifty-eight years, Carl Apfel has chronicled his beloved in every guise, as if in preparation for this volume, and he generously handed over his archives. Every snapshot of the grown Iris that illustrates her text, in which he doesn't appear with her, is most likely his work.

Christina Orr-Cahall, Roger Ward and Tracy Edling of the Norton Museum of Art made the photography possible by providing two unoccupied galleries at the crucial moment, enabling us to publish in tandem with their show. Thanks to Kent Allen Walton for his energizing spirit and expertise in the handling of mannequins, and to Pam Perry, Kelli Marin, Kevin Cummins, and Dan Leahy.

For advice and assistance, I extend my gratitude to Stéphane Houey-Towner of the Met's Costume Institute, and, for friendly generosity, to Caroline Hickman, Rita Konig, John Loring, Alexander Gaudieri, Linda Donahue, and Tom Matthieu.

For the comfort of working on another book with people I love and trust, I thank Connie Kaine, Thomas Neurath, Jenny Wilson and my countrywoman Karin Fremer of Thames & Hudson.

Eric Boman

"It's been a blast!"